Do You Belong in Journalism?

Do

Belong in

Edited

You Journalism?

Eighteen Editors Tell How You Can Explore Career Opportunities in Newspaper Work

HENRY GEMMILL and BERNARD KILGORE

APPLETON-CENTURY-CROFTS, INC.　　New York

Copyright © 1959 by The Newspaper Fund, Inc.

All rights reserved. This book, or parts thereof, must not be reproduced in any form without permission of the publisher.

PRINTED IN THE UNITED STATES OF AMERICA

Foreword

WHAT BUSINESS MAKES EVERYBODY ELSE'S BUSINESS ITS BUSINESS? It's the newspaper business—and those who successfully practice the profession of news reporting and editing consider it more than a business. It is somewhat of a science, uncovering truth. It is rather an art, telling its tales. It is very much a way of life; the newspaperman, with his quirk of curiosity, would consider almost any other career a bit dull.

Yet it is definitely not for everyone. How can a young person who is considering careers get some idea of whether he—or she—would be fitted for news work and would find it rewarding? How would he go about preparing himself for newspaper work, and how could he land a job?

Perhaps the best way to find answers would be to go around to a number of good newspapers and talk with expert newspapermen. This little book attempts to make such a pilgrimage for you. It contains the firsthand, down-to-earth opinions of eighteen newsmen in varied parts of the industry, from the president of the great United Press International newsgathering network to the editor and publisher of the weekly *Rock County Star Herald*, of Luverne, Minnesota. They were written in response to a letter containing nine specific questions. Many other responses from other able newsmen are hereby gratefully acknowledged; these opinions, too, were

FOREWORD

carefully studied before the ones to be printed in this booklet were selected as representative.

It will be noted that upon some matters the experts sharply disagree. But even these contradictions may be considered useful career information. For instance, some urge training in journalism schools while others scorn that as a waste of time. The moral: You can enter the profession by more than one road. Similarly, some editors say there is great opportunity for women in the newspaper field; others spurn them. Moral: A talented girl will probably have to shop around more than a boy before landing her first newspaper job, but that's no reason for any determined young lady to give up.

The preparation of this book was in large part inspired by a study made by Alvin E. Austin, who took a year's leave from his post as head of the journalism department of North Dakota University to investigate news staff recruitment problems across the nation. This research, supported by *The Wall Street Journal* and the Dow Jones Foundation, revealed some rather astonishing things.

It showed that many bright young people have the idea it's almost impossible to break into news work, while the fact is that 67 per cent of large and small newspapers surveyed consider "shortage of new manpower" to be one of their leading problems. It discovered that newspaper salaries, despite weak spots, have been improving faster than information about the gains has been getting around. It disclosed that a great deal of the vocational guidance information available to young people is inaccurate, out of date, or utterly confusing.

Attracting intelligent, capable, imaginative minds to the news profession, Professor Austin noted, "is a problem of importance to the whole American society. Newspapers always have needed the best minds available to perform their vital task of keeping the public informed. Never has this been truer than now, a time of scientific, social and economic breakthroughs."

HENRY GEMMILL
BERNARD KILGORE

Contents

Foreword   v

1. "Why are you considering it?" by John H. Colburn, Managing Editor of the Richmond, Virginia, *Times-Dispatch*   1

2. "The best way . . . is to start practicing it" by George W. Healy, Jr., Editor of the New Orleans *Times-Picayune*   5

3. "Curious about people and all the things in the world about him" by Frank H. Bartholomew, President of United Press International   8

4. "Nothing ever happens in a small town?" by Alan C. McIntosh, Editor and Publisher of *The Rock County Star Herald*, Luverne, Minnesota   11

5. "Not for the weak but . . . for the sensitive" by B. Dale Davis, Feature Editor of *The Detroit Free Press*   15

6. "The good ones must learn how to take a problem apart" by Erwin D. Canham, Editor of *The Christian Science Monitor*   20

7. "A professional calling, not a business or trade" by J. M. McClelland, Jr., Editor and Publisher of the Longview, Washington, *Daily News*   23

8. "I'd rather starve . . ." by Robert M. White, II, Co-Editor and Co-Publisher of the Mexico, Missouri, *Evening Ledger*   26

9. Newspaper people at work — a picture story   33

10. "For men who can't do anything else!" by James J. Kilpatrick, Editor of the Richmond, Virginia, *News Leader* 47

11. "If he wants to be a big shot . . . I try to discourage him" by Wallace Lomoe, Managing Editor of *The Milwaukee Journal* 51

12. "A more informal life, not tied to conventional office routine" by Michael J. Ogden, Managing Editor of the Providence, Rhode Island, *Journal* and *Evening Bulletin* 55

13. "A woman has to be more talented, more skillful, and more determined . . ." by Barry Bingham, President of the Louisville, Kentucky, *Times* and *The Courier-Journal* 60

14. "A strong belief in the principle of truth" by V. M. Newton, Jr., Managing Editor of the Tampa, Florida, *Tribune* 64

15. "Fiercely competitive in all of its aspects" by J. Edward Murray, Managing Editor of the *Los Angeles Evening Mirror News* 69

16. "Good newspapers are demanding and paying for higher quality work" by Kenneth MacDonald, Editor of the Des Moines, Iowa, *Register* and *Tribune* 73

17. "Should like people, reading, travel, new experience" by Howard C. Hosmer, Assistant Managing Editor of the Rochester, New York, *Times-Union* 77

18. "To arrive at facts and inform the public of them" by Coleman A. Harwell, Editor of *The Nashville Tennessean* 81

19. "The first requirement is a college diploma" by Charles Stabler, Managing Editor of the Pacific Coast Edition of *The Wall Street Journal* 84

Do You Belong in Journalism?

You often are given writing assignments, in the course of your school work. All of the short essays in this book were volunteered in response to a very similar assignment, given to leading newspapermen. Here it is:

> "Assume, if you will, this sort of situation: A young man at about high school senior age has asked *you* what about newspaper work. (By newspaper work, we mean editorial or news work—not sales or production.) What do you think about it as a career? What are the advantages and disadvantages? What's it like? Would you recommend it?
>
> "This is general. More specifically, how do you go about getting into newspaper work? What preparation do you recommend?
>
> "Even more specifically, this young fellow asks how can he tell whether he might be qualified for newspaper work. How can he judge or attempt to judge his own talents? How will he be judged by others later on?
>
> "One final query: What changes would you make in your answers if the inquirer was a high school girl instead of a boy?"

CHAPTER 1

"Why Are You Considering It?"

by JOHN H. COLBURN
Managing Editor of the Richmond, Virginia, *Times-Dispatch*

MY FIRST QUESTION TO ANY BOY OR GIRL SEEKING ADVICE ON A newspaper career is, "Why are you considering it?" That's not to discourage them. Rather, the question is designed to stimulate their thinking.

A newspaper career is an excellent vocation for anyone who can use and wants to use his head. A good newspaperman must be versatile. He must be able to cover the five-alarm fire or the Governor's budget message. He must know a great deal about consumer economics to handle both stories intelligently.

A five-alarm fire often can upset the economy of an entire community. It might, for instance, have destroyed a huge warehouse where a dozen merchants had stored inventory worth millions. It was insured only in part because the warehouse supposedly was fireproof. The ramifications—possible bankruptcy for some to booming business for new suppliers—spread far beyond the charred ruins of the warehouse.

The Governor's budget figures looked bleak and dull in their neat, orderly columns. But the reporter breathed life and excitement into them because he knew this: Some meant new taxes because expenses would exceed income; others meant a boom to architects and contractors because of new institution construction; others meant pay raises for schoolteachers or a modern juvenile detention home for delinquents.

DO YOU BELONG IN JOURNALISM?

What are the advantages of choosing such a career? First, the great personal satisfaction of creating something. In this case, creating through your own words a method of communicating information on an event or situation to someone else. Much of a reporter's job is distilling a mass of facts and figures and capsuling it for the husband and housewife so that they can better guide their own daily lives. The disadvantages are the hardships, frustrations and conflicts one encounters in any type of activity where you are dealing with unpredictable situations and human beings.

What's it like? There's plenty of excitement, plenty to stimulate even on the dullest days. The dull days can be made to come alive through your own initiative and planning. I find the longer I'm in it the more challenging a newspaper career becomes. As experience stimulates your mind to explore new avenues they open up broad boulevards of knowledge to be digested.

How to get into newspaper work?

Go to college. Concentrate on liberal arts your first two years. The subject emphasis should be on English, history, math and a foreign language. Later get a good taste of economics, philosophy and political science. Meantime, write, write and write. Write letters. Write digests of 100-150 words of your required reading. They will help you organize your thoughts, discipline your comprehension ability. Read newspapers. Note how they cover speeches. Write summaries of your class lectures in newspaper style. None of this work will be wasted if you decide on some other career.

During your freshman year in college, visit your local newspaper and apply for summer work as an office boy or editorial clerk. Applications should be made no later than January or February. The market is glutted with job-seekers in May and June. Having landed such a job, ask for the opportunity to accompany reporters on their beats on your days off. Keep your eyes open in the newsroom. If you can't type well, spend your spare time practicing on a typewriter to develop speed. Continue to write. Rewrite stories in the paper. If you have free time, ask the sports desk if you can help. Often they have routine items you can write. Ask questions. Learn the flow of the office routine and anticipate situations where you can be of help. Don't sit around waiting to be summoned.

If you find all of this gives you a certain, undefined sense of excitement,

— Photo by *Times-Dispatch* Staff Photographer James Netherwood, Jr.

John H. Colburn, Managing Editor of the *Richmond Times-Dispatch*, starts to sort the day's copy. In the background is Tom Robbins, newcomer to the sports department.

DO YOU BELONG IN JOURNALISM?

of "belonging," you have the makings of a newspaperman or woman. Your aptitude will be judged by how well you carry out your assignments, your attitude to those you come in contact with and the tactful initiative you show in trying to better your performance—and not by how vocal you are.

After a couple of summers as office boy or clerk, try to find a newspaper with a reporter-intern program. If you are in a college with a journalism school, you'll get experience on the school paper. A journalism background is no better than the school itself. Consult with experienced newspapermen before selecting your journalism school.

Keep this factor in your mind at all times: Many news sources try to "use" newspapers to put across some pet project or plan. Radio and television have added a vital new dimension to the communications field. In many cases they whet the reading public's appetite for information. This means more penetrative reporting. The reader no longer is satisfied with surface facts. He wants the background behind the facts to detail what they mean to him and his community or his neighbors.

There also are opportunities for both men and women in pictorial journalism. More than ever the picture must tell a story, not merely take up valuable white space to break up type. No mere technician who can snap a shutter will qualify for this job. The photo-journalist of tomorrow must have the educational background to analyze a story and the creative ability to develop a conception of it in pictures.

For the girls entering journalism, prepare yourself so that you are as good as, if not better than, the average man. Take any job you can get in the newsroom and then demonstrate by your performance that you are qualified for more responsible assignments.

I have personal interest in helping any high school youngster enter journalism. About thirty years ago, I attended a Hi-Y vocational meeting on journalism. The guest speaker, a copy desk editor, was kind enough to answer my questions after the meeting over a Coke at the corner drugstore.

CHAPTER 2

"The Best Way... Is to Start Practicing It"

by GEORGE W. HEALY, JR.
Editor of the New Orleans *Times-Picayune*

I THINK NO CAREER OFFERS GREATER OPPORTUNITIES FOR REAL service than newspaper work. Doctors can save lives and clergymen can save souls. Newspapermen have the power to save society.

Newspaper work has the advantage of giving the practitioner a broad opportunity to learn at firsthand about life and what makes a community live or wither. Generally speaking, the financial rewards are not as great as in some other fields, but this disadvantage does not apply to the most industrious or the most talented.

Newspaper work is like having an orchestra seat in the theatre where the attraction is REAL life.

The best way to get into newspaper work, in my opinion, is to start practicing it. If there is a neighborhood paper, a small town paper or a school paper, the person interested in newspaper work can volunteer contributions. If the editor of the respective papers is a real editor, he will recognize the contributor who is serious about wanting to do this kind of work.

If this opportunity is not available, there are several score journalism schools which offer excellent training. However, formal education in journalism should not be permitted to infringe on the prospect's studies in English, history, logic, ethics, basic mathematics and philosophy.

When a young fellow in journalism school comes to me and in-

— Photo by *Times-Picayune* Staff Photographer Tony Vidaco

George W. Healy, Jr., Editor of the New Orleans *Times-Picayune,* perches on a desk as he discusses the day's news.

"The Best Way . . . Is To Start Practicing It"

quires as to how he can tell whether he is qualified for newspaper work, I give him an opportunity to show me his resourcefulness and his ability to write by suggesting that he dig up a feature which he believes would be suitable for publication in *The Times-Picayune*. If he reads *The Times-Picayune* he will know what I mean by suitable for publication in our newspaper, and if he is reasonably resourceful he can submit copy which we can discuss, even if we cannot print it. I can tell him a few things on which he can base a reasonable judgment of his talents and I can assure him that the way he will be judged by others later on will depend largely on his ability to obtain information which is interesting to many of his fellow citizens, to write that information accurately, and to follow the precept that "The right of a newspaper to attract and hold readers is restricted by nothing but consideration of public welfare."

I do not believe that I would make any changes in my answers if the inquirer were a girl instead of a boy.

"Curious About People and All the Things in the World About Him"

CHAPTER 3

by FRANK H. BARTHOLOMEW
President of United Press International

FEW CAREERS CAN BE MORE SATISFYING THAN NEWSPAPER WORK for the man who is fitted for it. The man who is not should get out as quickly as possible, for his own sake and that of the profession.

A good newspaperman is curious about people and all the things in the world about him. He is interested in what people do and say and why. He enjoys reading because this enlarges his world of experience and knowledge. He has a desire to express himself in words and is willing to work hard to learn how to write clearly.

Besides a tremendous curiosity, the big thing, I think, is that he should *want* to get into the business. It seems to me that the most successful newspaper people are those who do it because this is what they want to do. Many of them started on their school papers and were "hooked."

Disadvantages include frequently odd hours, and if a man is to get ahead, as in any business, it involves a lot of work and study beyond office hours. A man may be away from home a great deal. To some people, odd hours and travel are attractive. A big advantage is the comparative freedom and responsibility (not freedom from responsibility) that go with newspaper jobs right from the start.

Putting it briefly, I would recommend a broad liberal arts program as a preparation, coupled with technical courses in journalism fundamentals, but nothing so elaborate as to shrink the liberal arts

— U. S. Navy Photograph

Frank H. Bartholomew, President of United Press International, still goes on news expeditions. Here, in flight helmet, he is boarding a radar search plane on the flight deck of U.S.S. *Intrepid* in the Caribbean Sea.

DO YOU BELONG IN JOURNALISM?

program too far. And the prospect should work on his student paper, to help his training and to help him evaluate himself.

I would make no changes in my answers for a girl, except to say that it is more difficult for her. Women lack some of the mobility of men, both before and after marriage. Regardless of the law, most people are reluctant to send women off by themselves in the early morning hours, for instance. And some hardships a man might shrug off wouldn't be fitting for a woman. Women tend to abandon their careers for marriage, and properly so, but a man is not faced with this choice. These factors tend to make employers hire only the exceptional woman applicant.

CHAPTER 4

"Nothing Ever Happens in a Small Town?"

by ALAN C. McINTOSH
Editor and Publisher of *The Rock County Star Herald*, Luverne, Minnesota

SITTING AT MY OFFICE DESK BATTING OUT SOME THOUGHTS ABOUT what I would tell a high school graduate concerning his future if he went into journalism, I have to ramble a bit.

I'd have to tell him he'd be about able to write his own ticket, but it would all depend on what he had to offer in "going the second mile."

Particularly in the country field or small city journalism he wouldn't be working a 37½-hour week. He would be unhappy if he wanted to live in an "ivory tower" because life would never be dull but it might be a struggle. Two of our newsmen had to leave their homes the other night in 15-below weather to go out and freeze after an eighteen-mile trip to a country fire . . . watching eighty-eight pigs burn up in a barn . . . the camera balky with the cold . . . then a couple of hours later a call that a small town was burning up about twenty-five miles away. (I double-checked and didn't send them; somebody had gotten over-panicky.) It may mean a 3 A.M. call from the sheriff that there's been a bad accident ten miles north on 75. It may mean sitting for long hours the first Tuesday night of every month covering the city council.

I think the fellow who starts in the smaller field and who works hard and shows ability will get ahead faster than his opposite number on the city papers. There are certain satisfactions and compensations that cannot be duplicated.

DO YOU BELONG IN JOURNALISM?

One of my men is an alumnus of a Washington paper who was a bit discouraged by the long row ahead. He came to us even though we told him "nothing ever happens in a small town." The first twenty-four hours he was here he covered:

1. The clean-up of a major safe-cracking job that has been written up since in the detective magazines as brilliant detective work.
2. A triple highway fatality.
3. The wild escapade of a teen-age murderer from Sioux Falls who brought a hostage along at gun point to this county, held a farm woman and family at bay and terrorized the county.

And this reporter said to me, "You said nothing ever happens in a small town."

The next six months, if you measure news in terms of tragedy or disaster, probably were terribly dull. But if you measure a newspaperman's job in terms of being the "moving finger of history" then it had satisfactions . . . helping promote a better community in which to live . . . helping record the joys and satisfactions of our community of readers.

I do say this: It is ten times tougher to be a good newspaperman in a small town or city than it is in a metropolitan area. It takes more courage. For instance, your best advertiser gets picked up for drunken driving . . . or a friend commits suicide. The problem of keeping your obligation to print the news fairly and fully and decently is not always easy. The city reporter can write any story with the knowledge that he may never see the party involved again. He can measure the story in terms of the size headline it will rate. We have to face up to writing that story with the knowledge we have to see those people every week the rest of our lives.

No acid known to chemists has the power to sear the human soul as does printer's ink, and sometimes it tests the courage of many a small-town editor to be a "good newspaperman."

The apprenticeship in journalism sometimes seems discouragingly slow, but the reward at the end of the row in tangible monetary success plus satisfactions of having produced something worthwhile for a community are great. The plugger who is willing to "plow the east 80" carefully will always get

— Photo by *Star Herald* Staff Photographer George Sauce

Alan C. McIntosh, Editor and Publisher of *The Rock County Star Herald*, at his working post.

DO YOU BELONG IN JOURNALISM?

there. The fellow who expects it all to be three-alarm fires and riot calls is not for us... he has to accept the drudgery and the heartaches which accompany the monotonous routine of a daily job.

One day I had received an application letter from a young man who outlined very distinctly what he expected; he emphasized he didn't care for any "sweeping out or menial work." That same day some baled paper had to be moved from the back entrance, so I said to Irid Bjerk, my news editor: "Come on, let's move that paper."

We were slipping and groaning—the mud was squishy and the paper was dirty—when I started to laugh. Irid said, "What's the matter with you?" I had just remembered the punk who said "no menial work."

There'll be a lot of menial work but a host of glorious satisfactions in journalism, in the small-town field. And there is always the chance of big success.

If I were a young man wanting to get into newspaper work I'd beat a path to a small city newspaper, daily or weekly, and offer to "do anything." Six months will tell whether you should be a chiropractor or a haberdashery clerk... or a newspaperman.

CHAPTER 5

"Not for the Weak But... for the Sensitive"

by B. DALE DAVIS
Feature Editor of *The Detroit Free Press*

WHEN I WRITE MY BOOK ON JOURNALISM, THIS ONE TO FOLLOW my books (all in the planning stage, of course) on Manolete, bass fishing, Winston Churchill, installation of washers on leaky faucets, James Oliver Curwood, duck hunting, and James Gordon Bennett, here's what I'm going to say:

Journalism is not for the weak, but it is for the sensitive. It is for the man (or woman) who has a feeling and compassion for his fellow man. The newspaperman today must have an understanding of the people at all levels of society. He must know what appeals to them, what offends them, what they understand, what they don't know, and what they don't want to know.

The successful journalist today must be a reasonably good writer, sincere, enthusiastic, possessed of a sense of humor, dependable, reasonably sober, responsible, open-minded, hard working, sound of judgment, curious. But above all he must be dedicated to the one thought that the job he is doing is the most important, most significant and most worthwhile of all jobs.

Probably the most undersold feature of newspaper work is the prestige that a newspaper job gives a man. He is a man looked up to. He is regarded as a man of wisdom, in the know, amazingly aware. He is singled out and, perhaps too often, flattered. Let the newspaperman beware of allowing this attention to get to him,

DO YOU BELONG IN JOURNALISM?

overwhelm him and becloud his work and personality. Many a downfall of a newspaperman can be attributed to his complete acceptance of this romancing, believing too deeply in his own press clippings.

The newspaper man today must beware of ruts, routine and, the curse of aging, ultra-conservatism. If a man is easily shaken by change—swift change—then newspapering is not his business. Perhaps this is the reason we have so often heard the newspaper business referred to as "the young man's game." As we age, we have the tendency to accept our established pattern as the way to do our job. But this cannot be allowed to happen in our business. We must keep questioning procedures, challenging techniques, keep "things stirred up," operate in a state of "organized confusion," as Basil (Stuffy) Walters, editor of the *Chicago Daily News* puts it.

Many newspaper people, I have found, are perfectionists of sorts. This leads to a frustration that is quite prevalent in our business. We shoot for what we know (or believe) is perfection in every edition or every page we produce and seldom do we quite come up to that goal of perfection. However, when we do hit this pinnacle (and it does happen on occasions) we go home with a rosy glow of satisfaction that no other job, no other profession under the sun, can offer.

These are some of the points (mostly, you will recognize, of philosophical nature) that I try to bring out when talking to a young person about newspapers as a career. For me, and I make every effort to pass this impression along to the youngster, journalism is the only career. It is a noble assignment, one to be proud of and, to be practical, one to profit from.

Some old newspapermen die broke. Some retire to Phoenix or Fort Lauderdale in a reasonable form of comfort. Some retire to journalism schools and, too often, forget what the years of practical experience have taught them. They start looking at journalism textbooks, realize that they are actually retired, and accept routine as the way to do the job.

This is not a general indictment of journalism schools. The schools are of considerable value to the aspiring journalist. I'm for them. I spent quite a bit of time in a couple myself! I tell the student considering journalism to take full advantage of the "laboratory" courses in journalism. These are the courses where the student actually writes newspaper copy, works on a

— Photo by *Free Press* Chief Photographer Tony Spina

Pipe-puffing B. Dale Davis, Feature Editor of *The Detroit Free Press*, assembles his "For and About the Family" pages with makeup man David Aird and Copy Editor Beverly Busch.

publication. I suggest that he might take one history of journalism course. Don't get bogged down with libel courses, ethics, foreign press, editorial writing, etc. Take all the copy reading courses offered. But above all, work at the job you hope to be doing when you get a degree. Don't major in journalism, I suggest. Dig into a social science, some psychology, much English and literature, probably a little philosophy in an effort to gain some insight into what you really are.

But to get back to practicality—money. Newspaper salaries on today's newspapers are not low. Ask any publisher. A few newspapermen get rich. Many live in a style that compares with the living standards of moderately successful men in many other professions. They probably are in the upper middle income bracket, as an average, or in the lower upper income bracket. Most newspapermen must resign themselves to the fact that they are always going to be "working for somebody"—seldom themselves. A very, very few have the funds or the courage to launch their own enterprise. Today's costs have put this habitual newsman's dream well beyond reach.

In the field of management, newspapers have been accused of neglecting and overlooking the training of executives. Much of this criticism is deserved. Today's newspapers generally are management thin. (Isn't this another selling point to the youth considering journalism? If he's got it, he can work knowing that there is room at the top for him. Room? There's a palace of opportunity at the management level.) Too many potential leaders are permitted to be lured to other allied fields. It is the job of newspaper executives today to develop talent, nurture it and then reward it accordingly—but reward only when there is definite assurance that the move is merited.

The starting newspaper pay may be called adequate, but hardly attractive enough to actively stimulate a fence straddler into the business. In many cases, those who accept the starting newspaper pay have that much-wanted quality of devotion to the business, otherwise they would have looked elsewhere for a livelihood.

How can a young man tell whether he might be qualified for newspaper work? Well, the young man can look at the long hours; the working conditions that leave something to be desired; the busy editor who, in keeping up his own production schedule, has little time to look around him and recognize possible talent; the uncertainty of his day's work. He can look at these things and then decide if he wants to join the most exciting business in the world; work with the most imaginative minds of the day; join the most stimulating people imaginable; become conversant with every thought of the day; face a challenge every hour; hold the immense respect of his fellow man; gain many, many intrinsic and intangible values.

If he looks at all these factors and decides, this is the business for me, then there's a pretty good chance he'll be a newspaperman.

A girl may not have an equal chance to succeed. But there certainly is room in our business—plenty of room—for the young woman who wants to work hard; avoid prattling and office politics; forget the production of the great American novel and vow to write simply, hard; approach her work seriously and not consider it a temporary break between college and maternity.

CHAPTER 6

"The Good Ones Must Learn How to Take a Problem Apart"

by ERWIN D. CANHAM
Editor of *The Christian Science Monitor*

I BELIEVE DEEPLY IN THE IMPORTANCE AND THE REWARD OF newspaper work as a career. The world has never more urgently needed capable men and women in the profession of reporting and explaining events and ideas. The times are complex and difficult. They require reporters and interpreters. Whatever disadvantages there are in the profession are far outweighed by the tremendous opportunities for genuine service. I cannot honestly be cynical about the business. It is of course unlikely that many newspapermen or women will earn very much money—but if they have real talent, they will be able to get by.

The young person should be sure he really wants to get into newspaper work. There are many dilettantes merely attracted by the so-called glamour. A true newspaper person must be driven by a compulsive urge. He has a call, or vocation. He will know whether or not he has it. If he doesn't have to write with all the urgency of a salmon going upstream in the spring, he had better stay out of the business!

Of course many more people will have the vocation and will get into newspaper work than will be able to stay there. There is not now economic opportunity for all of them. That is inevitable and not altogether undesirable. The structure of the profession is pyramidal.

— Photo by *Monitor* Chief Photographer Gordon N. Converse

Erwin D. Canham, Editor of *The Christian Science Monitor*, writes learnedly—as indicated by his background, shelf upon shelf of books.

DO YOU BELONG IN JOURNALISM?

As to preparation, of course a good solid general education is necessary. The student must learn how to think. He can acquire this capacity best by working with academic subjects which are most challengingly taught. The subject matter is not so important as the technique. Conceivably a newspaperman could learn how to think by taking apart mathematical problems just as well as he could by studying history or literature—perhaps better. Stern intellectual exercise is what he needs rather than merely knowledge.

There comes a time when vocational education is desirable provided it is taught rigorously enough. This is not always the case. In my experience there is no uniform pattern of education or formation of newspaper people. They come up in all sorts of different ways. But indispensably the good ones must learn how to take a problem apart and put it together again, and how to write.

I would make very little changes in these answers for a high school girl except to say that she will have a somewhat more difficult time than the boy. But if she has the true journalistic call and aptitude, she will come through —with decreasing difficulty as the years go by.

CHAPTER 7

"A Professional Calling, Not a Business Or Trade"

by J. M. McCLELLAND, JR.
Editor and Publisher of the Longview, Washington, *Daily News*

I THINK NEWSPAPER WORK PRESENTS MORE ATTRACTIVE CAREER opportunities now than ever before. It is just as interesting as ever, and provides just as many satisfactory experiences. In addition it pays better.

This work has a particular advantage for a beginner because it provides an early opportunity for recognition of ability. In many fields of endeavor it may take years for the good work of a person to come to the attention of those who are in a position to reward or recognize real ability. In newspaper work a person's output shows up in print right away where it cannot be missed. Other advantages include employment in a remarkably stable industry. The income of newspapers is generally quite even and the danger of losing one's job due to sudden and perhaps temporary slumps is remote.

Most lines of work are concerned with selling a product or a service. They involve dealing with the buying public. Not so with newspaper journalism. While it is true that newspaper journalists are helping to put together a salable product, their work is far removed from the world of commerce. Their task is to present the news as they see it. News gathering and editing is primarily a professional calling, not a business or trade.

If there is any particular disadvantage to a newspaper career it lies in the remote likelihood that a person embarking on such a

— Photo by *Longview Daily News* Staff Photographer Jan F

J. M. McClelland, Jr., Editor and Publisher of the *Longview Daily News*, is formal enough to wear a jacket in his newsroom—but informal enough to make it a sports jacket.

career will ever be in business for himself. Newspapers are fewer in number than in times past because they are more expensive to operate. To found a new newspaper or buy an existing one takes a great deal more capital than most men can expect to accumulate.

I would certainly recommend a newspaper career for any person who has an interest in people and their affairs, and who likes to work in the forefront of all that is going on, day by day, that is most interesting to most people.

How do you go about getting into newspaper work? The best way is to go to school and learn the fundamentals of journalism from competent instructors and good books. In short, go to a journalism school. Most journalism school graduates have an opportunity to get into newspaper work if they want to. A person might become a newspaperman without a journalism school education by getting a job as a copy boy or a cub reporter and learning the fundamentals on the job, but this is becoming the hard way whereas it used to be the easiest way.

How does a person tell if he is qualified? A newspaper journalist ought to have some talent for writing. A young person should know if he has such a talent by the time he is through high school. Did he get good grades in English composition? Did writing assignments in various classes come easy? If a person has a particular interest in some subject, such as sports, business, science, aviation, military, or the arts, he might be wise to aim toward a career in writing about his particular interest. All large newspapers now hire a variety of specialists who must have, besides a knowledge of how to observe and report, a thorough understanding of the subjects they are assigned to cover.

As for advice to girls, it would be much the same as to boys, except that a girl would have to be told that newspaper work is still considered by many editors to be primarily a man's job. In addition a woman has the traditional handicap of trying to convince a prospective employer that she will stay with the job and not be likely to give it up at any time for a career as a homemaker.

"I'd Rather Starve..."

CHAPTER 8

by ROBERT M. WHITE, II
Co-Editor and Co-Publisher of the Mexico, Missouri, *Evening Ledger**

HIGH SCHOOL SENIOR BOY OR GIRL: MR. WHITE, WHAT ABOUT newspaper work? Should I be interested in it?

RMWII: I'm the wrong fellow to ask. I'm prejudiced. I'd rather starve as the member of a newspaper staff than get ulcers and old in any other business in the world.

That's because I like news work. I'm in love with it. Take a look out there in the city room. See those people. They're the same way. Somebody once said that a newspaper is a jealous mistress. It is. It is both jealous and a mistress. Those people out there are in love with newspapering. They live, breathe and eat it. One reason is because it constantly demands their best effort in dedication to something far bigger than any individual, any single business.

And when I say they "live it" I mean they "live it." Maybe you have never noticed, but sometime try and find an old newspaperman. You will find men who are old in age in the newspaper business. But you will also find, only as the rare exception, the man who is old.

That's important because it may be that people don't grow old, staid, into vegetating lingering on this earth when they are doing something completely vital to them, something in which they

---

*On August 3, 1959, Mr. White became Editor and President of the *New York Herald Tribune.*

— Photo by *Ledger* Staff Photographer Vic **Hildebrand**

Robert M. White, II, Co-Editor and Co-Publisher of the *Mexico Evening Ledger*, occasionally joins a raid by state troopers.

believe, something they know is far bigger than themselves or "the company."

You see, a newspaper is a cause—a throbbing, moving cause far bigger than any employee or owner or corporation. The cause is the community itself—the town, county, nation. Newspapers are vital to democracy. A voter helps build a better democracy only by knowing as much as he can about the issue upon which he is going to vote. A newspaper's job is to supply that information in all the detail the voter needs, and in a way that the voter can glance at it, read it or study it just as carefully as he pleases, and when he pleases. Because this is true, it is why Thomas Jefferson said:

"The basis of our government being the opinion of the people the very first object should be to keep that right. Were it left to me to decide whether we should have a government without newspapers or newspapers without government I should not hesitate a moment to prefer the latter."

What I'm trying to say is that news work is important work.

Because it is, those people you see out there in that city room—reporters, editors—are accepted in this community and every community as of more than average importance. You can be sure when a reporter telephones a mayor and says, "I'm Jones of the *Ledger*," well, there isn't a mayor or a governor or a congressman . . . any official, who isn't immediately on his toes.

How many people in how many other professions have the automatic prestige a newspaperman has? Darned few.

But that coin has two sides.

I wouldn't want you to be a newsman if you were not going to be worthy of shouldering the prestige that comes with being one. You shoulder that prestige by being honest, responsible, a man of your word, totally dedicated, and big enough to rise above your own personal likes and dislikes. You must be big enough to report the news honestly, objectively and in a form that will be of most help to the voters, the people.

There's another reason I wouldn't want you to be a newsman, if you're guilty of it. That reason is this: If you like money, if money is your god, don't be a newsman.

Some people do worship money. It is their major motivation in life. If you are one of those people, don't be a newsman. It is too important a profession to have you in it.

"I'd Rather Starve..."

One of the best city editors I know has found a paycheck in his desk more than once when cleaning his desk once a year. The point is that he was too occupied with more important things to be bothered with a paycheck the day it was handed him.

And there is another point; he is paid so well that no one paycheck made much difference to him.

Pay is good, for newsmen. It constantly gets better. But newsmen are dedicated to causes above money. And they can afford to be. The reason is obvious when you understand the reason for newspapers.

You've heard that advertising income supports newspapers. Actually, for papers up to the fairly large ones advertising accounts for about 75 per cent of total income, the other 25 per cent coming from circulation. A look at this arithmetic leads most people to conclude that advertising controls newspapers.

What about that? Is it true? Nope, not at all. To say it is, is to underestimate the American merchant. He's a hardheaded businessman. He competes in a market of fierce competition. He has no dollars to spend regularly trying to dictate an editorial policy. The only reason he invests in newspaper advertising is to get back more than he spends for the ads.

How is that possible? There is one cause: the reader. If enough people read the merchant's ad, are interested in it, are moved by it to enter the store either to look at the merchandise or buy the merchandise, then that merchant's advertising dollar is working for him. When these readers turn customers, then the merchant profits from his newspaper advertising and will advertise more.

Because most people have the habit of shopping through newspaper advertising, merchants spend millions of dollars in newspapers every year. But the key to every dollar of that money is the reader. If a newspaper has the reader, then the merchant is going to get a good return on the money he invests in newspaper advertising.

So obviously, the key to good advertising income for a newspaper is loyal readers and plenty of them. Now, readers are people who buy the newspaper to read the news and ads—the news normally being their basic motivation or first interest.

Who gathers and writes this news?

DO YOU BELONG IN JOURNALISM?

Newsmen—reporters and editors.

That's why they are the heart of a newspaper. All other departments are important, but none would exist if people didn't buy the paper to read.

This is why top newsmen—the men who are the best in their field—earn so much money. Top writers, columnists earn more than many bank presidents or corporation executives. Of course, editors are equal in every way, including pay, to corporation executives.

But the point we want to make to you is this: Don't be a newsman if you're solely interested in money. If you are that kind of fellow, you'll be like the dog with a bone who saw his reflection in the water. Remember, he dropped his bone in the water in order to take the other bone away from the dog whose reflection he saw. Result: No bone at all. If you enter the news field watching the money more than your own talent and your ability to gather and write news, you'll probably end up a below average newsman without money or developed talent. In short, no bone at all.

If you want to work directly for money, enter advertising or the many other phases of the newspaper business where money is the primary target, the first concern. But if you want to be a successful newsman, enter the field devoting 100 per cent of yourself to developing your talents.

Incidentally, money can be lost, taken away from you, spent. But talent can't be lost; skill is unaffected by depressions; the habit of doing a dedicated job is better than dollars in your pocket . . . because talent, skill, dedication and good work habits guarantee money income.

I'm sorry, I've talked too much but I wanted to get down to brass tacks in answering your question.

High school senior boy or girl: Maybe I ought to think some more about news work. How can I find out if I like it? How can I prepare for it? How would I go about getting a job?

RMWII: Libraries have shelves of books about newspapermen—incidentally, the highest compliment a newspaperman can pay a woman in the news field is to call her "a good newspaperman." Read some of those books. They'll give you an idea. Reading is important to a newsman . . . don't think I ever saw a good one who didn't like to read. Those books will give you some ideas to think about. Maybe they will help you decide if you might like it.

"I'd Rather Starve..."

A still better way is to start working for your school paper. Take any job they'll let you have and, if they won't let you have one, then work your way into a job by helping some other student on the staff. Don't take no for an answer. Write stories and turn them in to the teacher in charge. Some way or another work your way in. You'll soon find out if you like digging up news and writing it.

Still better, see if you can get a job on your local newspaper doing anything. Maybe a summer job. If you can't start writing for them, ask the editor—he'll be pleased to be asked for advice—if you can try out. Tell him if he won't give you a job that you'd like to try to write some stories anyway. The kind of stories his staff may not find or cover. (Let me give you a tip. If you can't think of some story subjects yourself, read other newspapers in the library or at the newspaper office and pick out a few story ideas BEFORE you talk to the editor. Tell him you'd like to try to do a similar story for him.)

Meanwhile, keep college in mind. The best newsmen today have the help of a college background. Take some journalism but also take plenty of English, history, some science, music, art—everything you can get. A journalism degree will probably help you get placed after you have graduated. But a J-degree is not necessary. Many of us don't have them.

Let me put it this way, if you want to be a newspaperman, be one. Work for any newspaper you can—school, college, local paper. Or write for any publication. Write, write, write. Never get discouraged. The more you write, the better you will write. And never give up. You'll make it, and in making it establish habits that will be money in your bank. And be sure you read everything you can find on newspapering.

If you're not sure you want to be a newspaperman, read up on the subject. Talk with newsmen. Read papers, keeping in mind that some reporter went out and covered the story you are reading. If you're still not sure after you have done a good deal of this reading and talking, I believe I would not try to be a newsman. The good newsmen are as dedicated to being newsmen as good doctors are dedicated to being doctors. Some people have that dedication and some don't. If you are doubtful after you have researched the subject, I believe I would move on to other job possibilities—find one you like, love, can lose yourself in.

DO YOU BELONG IN JOURNALISM?

But, if you find newspapering is interesting, even fascinating, then you're lucky. Because it's a fascinating way of life—a wonderful, vibrant, exciting way to spend your days on earth and wish each day was longer. It's good pay, a lot of prestige... and living, really living.

CHAPTER 9

en news breaks sud-
ly, unexpectedly —
l the newspaper
st be as quick in
ponse as a fire de-
tment. Here City
itor Marshall Stross
the Dayton, Ohio,
rnal Herald takes a
ne call, consults his
p, and swiftly in-
ucts reporter Larry
ston.

— Photo by *Journal Herald* Chief Photographer Robert Doty

NEWSPAPER PEOPLE AT WORK
A Picture Story

Here are more than a score of pictures showing the broad range of a newspaperman's work. You'll find the editor at his desk, the reporter covering a story, a photographer making a news picture. You'll glimpse the inside of a newspaper office and its printing facilities. You'll find young people, some still in high school, already learning journalism. The photographs themselves, made by photographers on both large and small newspapers, show how news photographers and news editors, working together, can use pictures to tell a story. In this case, it's the story of newspaper work.

— Photo by *Evening Bulletin* Staff Photographer Charles T. Higgins

The news reporter interviews community and world leaders, but frequently it is more important to tell what ordinary people are thinking and doing. Labor reporter Harry Toland of the Philadelphia *Evening Bulletin* often does exactly that.

Aviation writer Charles Corddry of United Press International tries out a jet fighter plane on New York's Long Island. Like many reporters, he gets around—is just as likely to turn up at Thule, Greenland.

News reporting takes you to scenes of excitement — which might be a noisy political convention or, in this case, a quiet laboratory advancing the frontiers of science. Robert Toth (right), of the *New York Herald Tribune's* science staff, interviews Dr. Charles H. Townes, the Columbia University physicist who developed the MASER — a device which can pick up and amplify weak radio signals from distant reaches of outer space.

— Photo by *Herald Tribune* Staff Photographer Terence McCarten

News photographers must work as quickly and competently as reporters. Jerry Huff of the *Atlanta Journal* scurries to cover a wreck assignment. Hours later, he's likely to be recording a winning football touchdown.

— Photo by *Atlanta Journal* Staff Photographer Charles Pugh

The footloose reporter can wander far from home. Max Frankel, who covers Moscow for *The New York Times*, is seen shopping in Tsentralny Rynok, an open-air market, with his wife, Tobia, who does free-lance newspaper writing. Along with the day's vegetables they may get material for a story on the Russian cost of living. Both of the Frankels, incidentally, got into news work at college— Max as campus correspondent at Columbia, Tobia at Barnard.

— Photo by *Times* Staff Correspondent William S. Jorden

Covering the women's world can be done best by women reporters. Young Suzanne Clarke of the *Chicago Daily News* interviews Mrs. James Ward Thorne (left), who creates shadow boxes that are museum pieces. She gets interesting sidelights from Mrs. P. K. Wrigley, Mrs. Thorne's fellow worker at Chicago Woman's Exchange.

— Photo by *Star-Bulletin* Staff Photographer Warren Roll

News of the world at work takes reporters into the factory, out to the farm. Ben Thompson, of the *Honolulu Star-Bulletin*, takes notes in a pineapple field. Farmhand Alfred Remo is explaining how mulch paper, laid between the neat rows, cuts the cost and price of the fruit by discouraging weeds.

— AP Photo

Democracy works well only when the public is informed accurately and vividly of political maneuvers and governmental decisions. The newsman must fill this need—at the county courthouse, the town council meeting, the national political convention. This crowd of Washington correspondents is recording and analyzing a White House announcement.

The newsman must function not only with precision but with speed. These reporters break out of a Presidential press conference on the run, headed for telephones. At right are motorcycle messengers ready to rush cameramen's film to the newspaper photo offices.

— AP Photo

When the news story has been written, it needs a headline. If you think drafting a good one is simple, try it! It must be brightly; it must tell the story; it must be brief; each line must precisely fit. Here Wayne Goodman, of the Eugene, Oregon, *Register-Guard*, ponders one of these Chinese puzzles.

— Photo by *Register-Guard* Staff Photographer Phil Wolcott, Jr.

— Photo by *Star* Staff Photographer Francis Routt

The big modern newspaper's city room is efficiently engineered for its function of promoting the fast flow of breaking news—which means that it now has bright lights and fresh new desks, but retains all the exciting bustle and informal clutter of the old-time news shop. This is just one corner of the huge new newsroom serving *The Evening Star* in Washington, D. C. Reporters are seen in the foreground, and at left is the news department's phone switchboard. Beyond is the "master desk," where editors handle local, suburban, national and foreign news. Sports writers are in the extreme background.

39

Working conditions in the smaller newspaper shop can be just as modern as those offered by bigger publications. This is the city room of the Crawfordsville, Indiana, *Journal and Review*.

When a reporter anywhere in the country turns up an important or intriguing news story, it's likely to be picked up and moved to readers throughout the nation —and often to foreign lands. Enormous networks of leased wires and radio relays feed the news to teletype machines. Here's a row of them in one corner of the Associated Press headquarters in New York.

— AP Photo

— Photo by *Evening Tribune* Staff Photographer Theodore Lau

Putting out a newspaper starts as an intellectual exercise but can only be completed by a fast-paced manufacturing operation—and the news staff must pursue its words to the point where they become cold metal, locked in a page form ready for stereotypers and pressmen. Here news trainee James Hushaw (right) learns some tricks from Makeup Editor Forrest Lockard of the San Diego, California, *Evening Tribune*.

— Photo by *Citizen and Chronicle* Staff Photographer Jerry Kotlarz

Assistant News Editor Barbara Putscher looks over first copies of a section of the weekly Cranford, New Jersey, *Citizen and Chronicle* as they stream out of the press. Its capacity is eight pages and it turns out around 5,500 papers, usually in three sections and around twenty-four pages. Wearing the traditional pressman's cap, which he fashions from one of his own papers, is pressman John Lepinski, Jr. Tim Hayes and Fiske Martin (back to camera) check over the paper, too, before getting to work putting the sections together; both are high school students who work on Wednesdays—and Fiske considers it part of his training for entering journalism after college. This paper is among the many that offer job opportunities to students. Barbara worked in the society department during summers while in college. And the staff photographer who took this picture is an Upsala College student.

— Photo by *Cleveland Press* Staff Photographer Glenn Zahn

Huge plants are required to produce the nation's newspapers; each day they must "retool" to create a completely fresh product. Strolling out of the $12 million *Cleveland Press* building are Miss Carolyn Means, an Ohio University graduate who writes TV news, and Tom Boardman, who came up from the ranks of copy boys to become chief editorial writer.

43

News comes from high schools, too. Roy Dixon, a senior at the High School of Charleston, South Carolina, interviews a fellow student in the school corridor for a roundup of teen-age opinion. Roy's story will appear in the *Charleston Evening Post* in a special school section which is prepared by twenty-two student reporters and their adviser every other week.

— Photo by *Evening Post* Photographer William Jordan

If you think you might like to make a career of news reporting or editing, it's an excellent idea to get an advance sample of its tribulations and triumphs by joining the staff of your high school paper. Here students of Central High in Omaha, Nebraska, huddle as deadline approaches for printing *The Register*.

— Photo by *Omaha World-Herald* Staff Photographer Ed R.

— Photo by *Daily Citizen* Staff Photographer Bill Hopkins

Newspapers are eager to encourage high school students who are interested in news careers. The Tucson, Arizona, *Daily Citizen* takes on half a dozen of them as "observers" each summer, so they can accompany reporters on their rounds. Here Malcolm Terence (right) of Amphitheater High School is getting some tips over a cup of coffee from reporter John Barnett, who began his own career as a summertime observer.

Editors of high school publications often have opportunities to compare notes and hear professional newspapermen at press clinics and conferences. Here a few of the four thousand-plus who attend annual sessions of the Columbia Scholastic Press Association see Vernon Greene, artist for King Features Syndicate, demonstrate cartooning technique.

Young men and women prepare for careers in journalism with college courses. Alvin E. Austin, head of the University of North Dakota's journalism department, runs his classes like a newspaperman—from the "slot" of a horseshoe copy desk.

If you're heading for a news career, aim first at a top-notch college education—and get some practical experience on the campus newspaper. Here members of the sports staff of *The Decaturian*, a fifty-year-old student newspaper at Millikin University, in Ohio, are pasting up dummy pages. From left to right they are Tony Chamblin (who doubles as football halfback), Dave Lauerman, Tom Weyher and Fred McTaggart. Editors of this student publication can get professional guidance from a professional; their faculty adviser is Buryl Engleman, Executive Editor of the Decatur *Herald* and *Review*. But he is no censor—never sees a story before publication unless the editors wish to consult him.

Professional newsmen often give friendly advice to the young men and women who put out college publications. News Editor Edgar Orloff (left) of the *San Francisco News* answers questions posed by some of nearly a hundred student journalists attending a round table session sponsored by the California Newspaper Publishers Association. To attend the talkfest, where they also interviewed California's governor and toured newspaper plants, many of the college groups received financial assistance from neighbor publishers.

CHAPTER 10

"For Men Who Can't Do Anything Else!"

by JAMES J. KILPATRICK
Editor of the Richmond, Virginia, *News Leader*

WHAT DO I THINK ABOUT NEWSPAPER WORK AS A CAREER? I think it offers a wonderful career—for men who can't do anything else.

What are its advantages? Newspaper work permits a man with some creative instincts an opportunity to exercise those instincts; it offers the curious man a chance to satisfy his curiosity; it provides access to the seats of the mighty, for whatever such access may be worth; in the editorial end of the operation, newspaper work enables the conceited fellow to put forth his opinions with some dash and spirit.

What are its disadvantages? Low pay, the compulsive necessity of being respectful to politicians, the society of illiterates and bumpkins on one's beat, the sense of frustration that results from exhausting creative energies in writing that does not endure, and the managing editor's ulcers.

What's it like? In some ways, it's like every other job in the world: It is shaking the wife awake at 6:15 o'clock in the morning, going to the office with a bellyache, wondering why the children keep wearing out their Keds so fast, reading the morning paper, doing rewrites, getting the day's assignments, going out on the beat, seeing people, asking questions, getting answers, not getting answers, going to look for the answers, not finding the answers, making do with what you've got, writing copy, grousing at the

DO YOU BELONG IN JOURNALISM?

city desk, swearing at the proof room, finding pleasure in a good story, beating the opposition, explaining why you didn't beat the opposition, going home, playing with the children, cutting the grass, going to bed, and getting up at 6:15 the next morning to do it all over again. Anyhow, that's roughly what it's like as a reporter on a small city afternoon daily. And it's a wonderful life, for those who can't do anything else; and of course I would recommend it, for those who can't do anything else.

I keep saying "for those who can't do anything else," and I mean that literally. I am one of the last of the romantics in this preposterous business. I don't believe a young man ought to go into newspaper work unless he loves it so much that he can't do anything else. It is like getting married. If you could take some other girl to wife as easily, you ought not to marry the one you just asked. I put all this poorly because I am just knocking this out on a busy afternoon. Newspaper work offers a wonderfully satisfying career to people who think newspapers are wonderful; but newspaper work offers a great many irritations and frustrations to men who don't feel that way about newspapers.

The question is sure to come up: What of going to journalism school? For the talented young man, I can't imagine anything more wasteful of his time. Journalism schools may have their place in training advertising copy writers, ad designers, typographers, and journalism teachers, but I think they are not worth much in training reporters, editorial writers, or good desk men.

I would suggest to your bright high school boy, eager for a career in newspaper work, that he pick out an excellent liberal arts college, blessed by a few crack men in English, philosophy, history and literature, and that he go there for three years. Then I would suggest that he go to a law school for another year, and try to work things so that he emerges with an A.B. degree. I would want him to study law because so much of a reporter's time is spent covering judicial or quasi-judicial tribunals, and because the techniques of research involved in working up a lawsuit are similar to those involved in working up a definitive newspaper story or series of articles. The questions a lawyer learns to ask are pretty much the same searching questions a newspaperman learns to ask. In the summers, I would have this lad work on small papers as a fill-in. He could learn to write acceptable headlines in forty-five minutes

— Photo by *News Leader* Staff Photographer L. J. Patterson

James J. Kilpatrick, Editor of the *Richmond News Leader,* meanders through the newsroom exchanging ideas with the staff.

DO YOU BELONG IN JOURNALISM?

under a good slot man; he could learn the necessities of typography and the printing process in a week; any reasonably competent city editor could teach him more in any given month of August about the techniques of news writing than a journalism professor could teach him in the fall and spring semesters.

How would I judge a high school boy's aptitude for newspaper work? I would have him write a thousand words on something and read it. You could tell from a thousand words whether he had any feel of language, whether he knew a subjunctive construction, whether he thought in pedestrian terms, whether he could spell.

If this were a girl inquiring about a newspaper career? I would tell her to go study nursing, modeling, the techniques of singing contralto, the making of spaghetti sauce, and the breast feeding of infants, all of which women do better than men. I have known maybe half a dozen good newspaperwomen; the rest have been ornamental hacks, and sometimes not even ornamental.

CHAPTER 11

"If He Wants to Be a Big Shot .. I Try to Discourage Him"

by WALLACE LOMOE
Managing Editor of *The Milwaukee Journal*

ON OCCASION I TALK TO BOTH BOYS AND GIRLS OF HIGH SCHOOL age about the possibilities of newspaper work. Over the years my line of answers has changed somewhat, due to what I consider changing conditions.

I do recommend newspaper work as a career if the boy seems to have a basic idea as to what he wants to do. I try first to find out in what he is interested. If he wants to be a big shot, make a lot of money, use it as a stepping stone to politics or influence, I try to discourage him. If he wants to learn things and tell about them, I encourage him. I point out that he will be well paid and that the chances for more pay are increasing all the time, but that he should consider the broader field of publishing and possibly eventual ownership if he is interested in the highest financial returns in the business. (Right here I seem to be talking against some of my own ideas because I deplore the statements of many newspapermen that editorial people are very poorly paid.) What I try to point out is that while it is not a get-rich-quick line of work, there is more than adequate pay if the person can make his way ahead in the field. I also try to correct him of any ideas he may have picked up from the movies or fiction about the free and irresponsible, glamorous type of newspaperman.

I believe that a good newspaperman should have both a wide

range of knowledge and a responsible attitude toward society. I try to question the young men along these lines. I probe for interest in good writing, because that is basically most important. I try to point out the varied opportunities in the newspaper business. I have stressed in recent years the growth of parts of newspapers that are not specifically tied in with spot news, police, courts and immediate politics. I point out the need for curiosity and an inquiring mind, interest in people and what they do, and the processes of our complicated world.

When they ask what they should take up in college I do not stress complete journalism courses. I point out the value of basic reporting and editing courses, history of the press and possibly some of the legal aspects of it. I advise against too many detailed courses in such things as typography. the mechanics of the business, etc., unless they think they might go into the weekly or suburban field where they require such special knowledge. I tell them that if they are sure they are going into newspaper work, not to waste too much time on other communications subjects such as TV, magazine and specialty courses. Incidentally, I think that too many of our universities take a shotgun approach to all communications, but apparently that is unavoidable, especially in land grant schools where they are required to teach almost anything that is asked.

I think a college education for a good journalist should include economics, history, some good basic sociology and in these days perhaps more science than formerly. The top journalist should be a generalist.

If the prospect wants to work toward management in news departments, he should add some courses along business lines and management procedures. (For here, I believe, is one of the big weaknesses of our business. We're still bringing up reporters and copyreaders into management ranks without adequate management philosophies. Our news rooms are badly outdated in basic organization: do we still need old-time telegraph editors, city editors, etc., or do we need trained organizers who can take a fresh look and draw some new lines?)

I advise working after college on a *good* small newspaper to get a fast rounding out that is hard to get on a metropolitan newspaper. That provides a growing experience, which is not always possible at first on a big paper. I also

— Photo by *Journal* Staff Photographer Arthur Uhlmann

Wallace Lomoe, Managing Editor of *The Milwaukee Journal,* peers over the shoulder of News Editor Harry Sonnenborn as they decide how to display stories on the front page.

DO YOU BELONG IN JOURNALISM?

tell them that even so they must have patience and that they cannot hope to be writing world-changing editorials before they learn the rudiments.

I tell girls basically about the same thing but I caution them that their field is a little narrower. I find that most girls do not want to work on the specialties which women generally cover on newspapers. Very few actually are as serious as the boys about full careers. On the other hand, there are some who actually are more creative and imaginative and are good writer prospects. They should be encouraged because there will always be a place for them on good newspapers.

Reverting to the question as to how a young man can assess himself, I think he can tell somewhat by what he is doing in high school. If he is interested in his writing subjects, or is active on the school newspaper, or if he is trying to make contacts with his city's newspaper to cover sports or other activities, he has a genuine working interest. If he dreams of foreign correspondence, novel writing, etc., he had better take a little closer look at himself because they may be only dreams. He should consider whether he is resilient and aggressive enough to meet people and get what he wants.

CHAPTER 12

"A More Informal Life Not Tied to Conventional Office Routine"

by MICHAEL J. OGDEN
Managing Editor of the Providence, Rhode Island, *Journal* and *Evening Bulletin*

THE FACT THAT I AM STILL IN NEWSPAPER WORK AFTER TWENTY-five years might indicate I think well of it. Of course, it could indicate that I was too lazy to get out of it or that nothing else had turned up over the years to lure me elsewhere. But the most honest answer would seem to be that I have enjoyed it and have never given serious thought to any other work.

Not everyone who enters newspaper work will become a managing editor, but then, not everyone who enters the teaching profession becomes head of a university, nor does every lawyer become a member of the Supreme Court. In one, like the other, there may be glory enough, pleasure enough, self-satisfaction enough, achievement enough, at other levels.

Advantages? A major one, if you're suited to the field, is that you do for work what others do for fun. Reading, writing, research, meeting people, traveling, specialization in an art or a science—all of these are a part of newspaper work at the same time that they may be hobbies for, say, a businessman.

It is a more informal life, not tied to the conventional office routine. A good editor of a good newspaper will recognize that the reporters he has working for him are responsible, adult citizens; he will assign a chore or—and this will happen as often as not—give the go-ahead to a reporter on an idea of the reporter's own.

DO YOU BELONG IN JOURNALISM?

Then the editor will step out of the reporter's way and let him produce.

This is not to say that there is not also a routine, or that there are not frequent times when a rewrite man is under pressure and harassment to produce a story swiftly (which is a challenge of its own). But, by and large, on many of the major efforts of a serious-minded newspaper, a reporter is often given a job to do and he is free to do it, subject to such advice as he may seek while so engaged, and subject to searching examination of his job when he has completed it.

Certainly as much as, possibly more than, in other fields, the workaday atmosphere is stimulating and—why decry it?—fun. A camaraderie exists among reporters and among reporters and their editors to an extent not generally matched elsewhere.

The physical nature of the average city room itself, the ebb and flow of the visitors (offering no small cross section of human nature), the openhanded relationships between newspapermen and all manner of people in all walks of life play a part in this. Then, too, despite inroads and attacks, there is still such a thing as the power of the press, and this leaves its mark on the practicing newspaperman.

That's the exhilarating side. There's another, naturally—where tedium can be the order of the day for weeks on end (but never forgetting that somehow, sometime, there comes a break when the intervening boredom is forgotten). There are chores to be accomplished, and not all papers at all times can leave the newspaperman free to concentrate solely on his large thoughts. There are minor obituaries to be handled, notices of advance meetings to be written, club and events calendars, lists of servicemen, a thousand and one household details which are the very backbone of most newspapers' coverage, and which, above all, must be handled accurately.

To this point I have made no mention of money. It may be that anyone who has read this far and finds the question—"All very well, but what about salary?"—gnawing at him, ought to look elsewhere. For, despite the advances made in pay in the last twenty years, one still should enter newspaper work reasonably certain he will never become *very* wealthy.

As a good competent reporter on a good solid newspaper, the newspaperman might expect to make as much as a good competent professor at a uni-

— Photo by *Journal* and *Evening Bulletin* Staff Photographer Winfield I. Park

Michael J. Ogden, Managing Editor of *The Providence Journal* and *The Evening Bulletin*, is a typical working newsman—shirt sleeves rolled, collar open, pencil on ear, prepared to make ten important decisions in five minutes.

versity of good repute. The same can be said for a good desk man or makeup man. As with the professor, possibly even more so, there are means of making additional money from his writing or editorial talents. The newspaperman today will have the time if he has the will. This was not always the case a generation ago. Today the five-day, forty-hour week is fairly standard on newspapers, as are, in many cases, pension plans and insurance benefits.

There is more money to be made within the profession itself, depending on the job achieved. If—and most newspapermen do—one stops just short of being a publisher, he might hope to equal the pay of, say, a Cabinet official. Beyond that, subject to the few exceptions on the largest American papers, there is presumably nowhere to go except into the office of publisher and, by that time, he is drifting away from straight editorial and news work.

It could be put this way: Newspaper work could be recommended as a career if your spirit moves you to be interested in more than the surface of the world about you, if you have some interest in putting ideas on paper, if you enjoy people, if you can abide a certain amount of drudgery, if you have an innate feeling for the proper word and a sense of discomfort when the improper one appears, if you have a temperament that impels you not to take things for granted so that some official handout statement will not appear to you as a divine revelation but simply as a springboard for further independent investigation.

A lad seeking to judge his own talents can examine himself on these scores. He can be judged—and may well be judged by others later on—by the breadth of his interests. Then, there is no denying personality would have an effect on any prospective employer. The youth might be judged on as little, seemingly, as his ability to get up in the morning. He may be judged on a notorious inability to get names correct or street addresses straight in a story. He may be judged on the slight glaze that comes into his eyes when he is asked to take on a burdensome checking job in a staff-wide investigation.

There are such things as enthusiasm, spirit, willingness, and enterprise, which are not always cliches even in as supposedly hard-bitten a business as newspaper work.

The ways of getting into newspaper work are almost as numerous as there are jobs on newspapers. A general college education is eminently desirable.

"A More Informal Life, Not Tied to Office Routine"

Journalism school may help in garnering introductions to newspapers and newspaper personnel managers, but the school is not an indispensable requisite. Specialization is not necessary, but if there is a field in which the student is particularly interested, a major in it will do him no harm and may lead to a newspaper field that he will want to make his life work.

Best bet for the young man choosing his first job would be whatever enables him to achieve the broadest possible base in newspaper work. This could be on a small paper, it could be on the state or suburban staff of a larger newspaper, or it could be on the metropolitan end of a wire service wherein he could handle such elemental matters as police and court work. The small paper or the state-suburban staff of the larger one would be preferred. In either case, you can try your wings in many ways, from covering town meetings to chasing the fire wagons.

I could think of nothing different to say to a girl inquirer than to a boy, other than to append a warning that things would be many times as tough for her as the boy. Few editors, given a choice of apparent equals or even a slight weighting in the girl's favor, would incline to the girl. Editors still have a reluctance to take women on general assignment or work that could lead them at night into dangerous territory. There are, in addition, biological factors, current and potential, that sway editors' thinking. It would probably be well for the girl to have all the qualities outlined for the boy, but to have them many times over. Then, as Bernard Baruch once said in another connection, she might have a Chinaman's chance of making the grade.

"A Woman Has to Be More Talented, More Skillful, and More Determined..."

CHAPTER 13

by BARRY BINGHAM
President of the Louisville, Kentucky, *Times* and *The Courier-Journal*

ASSUMING THAT A HIGH SCHOOL SENIOR HAS ASKED MY ADVICE ON going into newspaper work, I would urge him first of all to give the matter very careful thought and not be misled by any false notion about journalism he may have gained from TV, the movies, or works of fiction.

Newspapering for the average man is not a glamorous or romantic career. Only a few journalists with special training and talents get to be foreign correspondents, or highly paid columnists, or Washington bureau chiefs, or famous editors. The great majority spend their newspaper lives doing hard, fast and demanding work in an office, for pay that is not handsome in relation to the amount of education and constant self-improvement the work requires.

Journalism is not, on the other hand, the tough, rowdy, bibulous profession it used to be (if indeed it ever was to anything like the extent of the popular myth). It is a responsible profession, with standards that are continually rising. It requires not only a sound basic education, but an ability and a willingness to go on learning right through the working years. The handling of news, in every aspect of the job, grows more complex all the time as America moves to the center of the world stage.

Journalism is not the job for a person who is primarily concerned with financial security, community prestige, or with an opportunity

"A Woman Has to Be More Talented, Skillful, and Determined"

for literary self-expression. It is a demanding and imperious profession. Its dynamic quality, which makes it fascinating to those who have a true taste for it, can also make it absorb all a man's time and mind and energies to the point of exhaustion.

Would I recommend it to a high school senior? Only on the basis that some people have been known to recommend marriage: It is something to be done only if you are so much in love that you cannot possibly do otherwise. People do fall in love with newspaper work, and in most cases the infatuation lasts for life. They are the only people who should be in the profession from the start.

To a young man who wants to prepare for newspaper work, I would urge four years of the stiffest, best-rounded liberal arts college training he can possibly manage. I much prefer this to the vocational type of training. If he feels a need for academic courses in journalism, I would recommend that he wait and take them at a good graduate school.

During his undergraduate years, he should dwell heavily on the "content" courses, and forget the easy courses around the fringes of college life. He will need extensive training in English, not omitting the basic tools of grammar, spelling and punctuation, which he may have learned in only a slipshod way in his earlier school years. History, government and economics are good fields for the preparation of a journalist. Latin is decidedly helpful in forming a clear and precise use of English. Modern languages have a broadening effect on the mind, and the physical sciences offer an intellectual discipline that is very useful.

There is almost no serious college course, in fact, that will not prove of some specific value to a newspaperman in our age of protean news development. Most papers, furthermore, are training specialists in such varied subjects as medicine, education, labor activities, and the fine arts. College work can lead to good opportunities in these fields of newspaper coverage.

If the high school senior asks how he can know if he is qualified for newspaper work, my answer would be that he cannot possibly be qualified at that stage of his development. It helps if he has shown some facility for writing and a respect for the handling of language. His potentialities as a journalist, however, depend primarily on his determination to improve on whatever talent he

— Photo by *Courier-Journal* Staff Photographer Jim

Barry Bingham, President of the *Louisville Times* and *The Courier-Journal*, goes to the composing room to check type in the page form.

"A Woman Has to Be More Talented, Skillful, and Determined"

may have, his ability to absorb knowledge and make it his own as contrasted to an ability merely to get good marks in his courses, and a real spirit of dedication that will drive him to seize every advantage at his disposal in preparing himself for a ruthlessly demanding profession.

If the boy feels the need of some objective evaluation of his potential ability as a future newspaperman, he can probably get some help from the English teacher he most respects. He might also benefit from talking to the managing editor or some member of the news staff on his home-town paper, making it clear that he is not seeking an immediate job, but that he wants guidance on preparing for his career. Most newspapermen would be willing to see such a boy, by appointment, and give him some practical advice.

If the high school senior asking my advice were a girl instead of a boy, I would offer much the same counsel, but with even stronger emphasis. Women have better opportunities in journalism today than ever before, but there is no use pretending that they are opportunities equal to those of men. A woman has to be more talented, more skillful, and more determined than a man to make her mark in this field. If she is willing to make a career in the handling of women's news, she will find the opportunities somewhat easier. If she is determined to compete with men in the general news field, she must be prepared to show a really superior performance.

Advancement may be somewhat slower for women and salaries even less munificent. But as to the most important factor, the human satisfaction to be gained from a job, I think a woman can find every bit as rewarding a life in journalism as a man can.

"A Strong Belief in the Principle of Truth"

CHAPTER 14

by V. M. NEWTON, JR.
Managing Editor of the Tampa, Florida, *Tribune*

I MIGHT SAY AT THE OUTSET THAT I DO HAVE HIGH SCHOOL BOYS and girls come into my office and ask questions. Always I take the time and trouble to discuss our profession with them.

I point out that personally I think newspapering is the finest possible career for the young person in that (1) it offers a great challenge, (2) it is a life of public service, and (3) it offers the great self-satisfaction of creativeness. But it does not, I warn, offer the opportunity of great riches. To offset this, it yields a full life of no boredom, which, in my opinion, is worth all the riches in the world. It is the writing of history in the making, the moving study of the human being at his worst and at his best, the great satisfaction of constantly being a part of life, not only in the raw but in its sublime form, rare as this may be and even if it consists of the defeat of man on principle.

A newspaperman, I tell these youngsters, is concerned with man; with what man does and does not do; with what man says and thinks; and, more important, he spends his life in the service of man. And there is no more interesting creature on this globe of ours than man.

The newspaperman duly records man's birth; he hovers backstage as man graduates from school; he ushers man down to the altar of matrimony; he listens in as man pleads his cause in the divorce court; and he serves as a pallbearer at man's funeral. And in between, he scribbles madly in taking notes of man's triumphs and tragedies in his material life.

What a grand life!

In every case, the youngster responds by telling me that he is intrigued with the idealistic challenge of our profession, that riches mean nothing to him, that he is eager to devote his life to the challenges of newspapers. Yet, in recent years, I have noted that a change takes place during his college years. I do not know whether this is due to the cynicism of the professors, to the new style of progressive education, or to the inroads of our expanding age of materialism. But I do know that, whereas our high school graduates are imbued with the idealism of life, our college graduates are more concerned with security.

I know this firsthand because each September I hie myself to Gainesville and interview some dozens of applicants for the *Tribune* journalism scholarships at the University of Tampa. I have been appalled at the thinking of these young collegians simply because in my day, the class of 1926 doffed their sheepskins and set forth to change the world for the better and never mind security.

Perhaps I have fallen into the ancient ways of one generation criticizing its succeeding generation, but recently I asked two young journalism graduates of Florida State University at Tallahassee, now on my staff, if they had ever heard of John Peter Zenger.* Each replied no and wanted to know who was the gentleman.

In recent years I have been leaning more and more to the thinking that a good liberal arts education is better than a journalism curriculum as preparation for a newspapering career. In addition to teaching our young college graduates spelling and the simple principles of English grammar in our news room, we have to spend about three years in teaching them the fundamentals of American government. It is rare that we get a college graduate who has the faintest idea of the place of the justice of peace court in our structure of

---

*The acquittal of John Peter Zenger in 1735 following his imprisonment and trial on a charge of publishing "seditious libels" in his newspaper, the *New York Weekly Journal*, was the first significant step towards establishing a free press and freedom of speech in America.

— Photo by *Tribune* Staff Photographer Rosco

V. M. Newton, Jr., Managing Editor of *The Tampa Tribune*, talks with young reporters June Wade and Art Smith.

"A Strong Belief in the Principle of Truth"

justice or of the great network of federal bureaus that stretches over our land and which puts a finger on the life of every American citizen. As for a governmental budget, why you might as well launch into the pure Greek of a Plato essay. And as for the history of mankind, which is still the basic principle of the reporting on newspaper front pages, our young collegians must start out without the faintest knowledge of what man has done in the past, even though there is the probability that he'll do the same thing today.

I used to think that a year's training on a weekly or a very small daily was the ideal beginning for a college graduate in journalism on the grounds that, having to do everything, he would learn far more in a shorter time than he would in the departmental ways of a big daily. But today, after some ten years in the fight for freedom of information, I am not so sure. I have found too many small papers, whose printing shops have contracts with government, prefer the ways of slanted reporting. I am convinced that this is not good training for the young journalist and I believe also that this has a direct bearing on why so many newspapermen are turning to the easy virtues of public relations.

What I am trying to say is that any young person with the proper personal qualifications for journalism can get a running start in his career by a liberal arts education, with due emphasis upon history, plus a great knowledge of and belief in the ideals of our profession. I can assure you that there are many editors who will listen to him and gladly provide the opportunity.

The personal qualifications are simple to state but are not so simple in actual practice. A bright, searching mind, of course, is an essential. But going with this must be a strong belief in the principle of truth, and the best newspapermen usually have at least a slight outrage at the injustices of life in their souls, whether or not they portray it in their stories. A man who is not stirred by life in general should stay out of the profession. And if you prefer popularity to respect, by all means get into public relations. An honest editor cannot win a popularity contest. But the greatest prize of all, the respect of his fellow man, awaits him.

As for women, I am not sure that I am competent to discuss them. I had experience with them during the war years and now that lovely peace is upon us, even though it is a troubled peace, I manage to find men for my news staff. The women's department, of course, is another matter. But few young women are interested in making a career of the women's department. Now that they have donned man's pants, they think newspapering is chasing ambulances, etc., and that is what they want—glamour and more glamour. Some of the greatest news stories originate in the off-the-record statements of the great. But man being man and woman being woman, man rarely opens up his innermost thoughts to woman, and vice-versa. Perhaps this is a lack of trust of one sex in another but it is primary and as long as man is running the affairs of man, it will take man to report those affairs properly.

Yet there is a great field in women's reporting, even though most of the sweet young things shy away from it. I don't believe women like each other. Anyway, the nation's women's pages are undergoing a change today; women's news is being broadened considerably beyond the wedding, and a good many newspapers are prepared to pay considerable money for the services of female editors of women's pages. I have discussed this with a number of high school girl graduates, but they simply show no interest. I point out that in Florida elections, 53 per cent of the vote is female and therefore women's pages need the touch of female political reporting, along with the reporting of the female's broadened approach to modern life, now that we have given her freedom. But it's wasted breath. The sweet young things want no part of their sisters; they want only their murders bloody, and preferably male.

CHAPTER 15

"Fiercely Competitive in All of Its Aspects"

by J. EDWARD MURRAY
Managing Editor of the *Los Angeles Evening Mirror News*

ANSWERS TO HYPOTHETICAL QUESTIONS OF A HIGH SCHOOL SENIOR:

Q. What do you think about newspapering as a career?

A. For a man or woman with the necessary natural aptitude, who is willing to acquire the essential qualifications of education and experience, newspapering offers an extremely rewarding career.

Q. What are the advantages?

A. Among the advantages are:
- —the idealistic satisfaction of helping the democracy function by helping to keep the people informed, by exposing corruption.
- —the satisfaction of keeping abreast of news, of knowing what's going on in the world, of being well informed as part of one's job. For those with the gift of real curiosity, this is important.
- —the considerable prestige in the community that goes with the two foregoing.
- —monetary reward in keeping with competence. Despite a bad press to the contrary, good newspapermen are fairly well paid.

Q. What are the disadvantages?

A. Newspapering, thank God, is fiercely competitive in all of its aspects. Among other things, this means good paying jobs are hard to come by and sometimes hard to hold; newspapers themselves are constantly threatened by allegedly more glamorous if less efficient information media, and this tends to make newsmen feel insecure, sometimes causes them to lose their jobs; economic and political ownership pressures often force newsmen in the direction of compromise with the highest principles and ideals, and this detracts from the satisfactions mentioned earlier.

Q. What is newspapering like?

A. It offers great variety, depending on the size of the newspaper, the size of the town, and the kind of newspaper job. The only way to find out what newspapering is like is to talk to newsmen doing different jobs.

Q. How do you go about getting into newspaper work?

A. Several good ways. Start as a carrier boy. Try to get a newspaper job as a copyboy or whatever during the summer months while in high school. Take journalism in college and try to get a newspaper job during vacations.

Q. What preparation do you recommend?

A. First, as much education as possible: i.e., in the usual formal way in school and college; through broad experience; through as much travel as possible; and by omnivorous reading. Second, as much writing of the English language as possible in a simple, concise style aimed at communicating meaning. Personally, I think a liberal college education is now requisite to intelligent newspapering. And it must include science as well as the humanities.

Q. How can I tell whether I'm qualified?

A. Are you curious about people and all they do? Are you idealistic in the sense of wanting to do some good in the world? Are you looking for a fiercely competitive occupation? Do you have a way with words; good word skills in grade school, good vocabulary, good articulation of what you want to say? Do you take satisfaction in being informed on many subjects?

If your answer is "yes" to these questions, you may have the makings of a newspaperman. If your answer is "no" to these questions, you still might make a newspaperman. There's no sure way to tell. As in other fields men and women who eventually become proficient occasionally begin by accident, or without seemingly necessary qualifications and interest.

Q. Would your answers be different to a high school girl?

A. Not much. There is still some prejudice against women in newspaper-

— Photo by *Mirror* Staff Photographer Nelson Tiffany

J. Edward Murray, Managing Editor of the *Los Angeles Evening Mirror News* (right), joins his picture editor in selecting the best shot of a spectacular news event.

ing. Women have the disadvantages of homemaking and childbearing to avoid or accommodate. Finally, men can do more things in newspapers than women. But there is a growing place for women in newspapering.

CHAPTER 16

"Good Newspapers Are Demanding and Paying for Higher Quality Work"

by KENNETH MacDONALD
Editor of the Des Moines, Iowa, *Register* and *Tribune*

I DON'T KNOW HOW ARTICULATE I AM WHEN HIGH SCHOOL SENIORS ask me about newspaper work, but I try to give them a realistic appraisal and, to those who indicate genuine interest, a wholehearted recommendation. I believe some editors who remember too well the days of extremely low salaries are needlessly gloomy about the advantages of a newspaper career. I know some editors who delight in lecturing young men and women on how hard newspaper work is. It isn't easy, but I question whether it is harder than any other occupation which requires a man to use his brain as well as his legs.

I can think of few careers which offer as wide a range of opportunities to the person with ability who is willing to prepare himself. The opportunities seem to me better and more varied now than ever before, because good newspapers are demanding and paying for higher quality work, and because good newspapers are realizing the need for more specialization among their staff members.

I tell high school seniors that a newspaper job is important, interesting, challenging and rewarding.

It is important because people depend on newspapers. Our type of democracy wouldn't function without them. What kind of understanding people have of their community and nation and of society

DO YOU BELONG IN JOURNALISM?

generally, what values they hold, depend in large measure on what they read in newspapers. People do get information from other media, of course, but I think the printed word in the daily newspaper is still paramount. The newspaper is an important factor in determining the political, intellectual, social and economic climate of the region in which it circulates.

A newspaper job is interesting because newspapermen work where things are happening. Another way to say this is that the newspaperman has the opportunity that few people have to be a part of the significant activity of the time and place in which he happens to live. Whatever human endeavor interests him most—politics, science, education, the arts, agriculture, government—journalism offers the opportunity to be a part of that activity by studying it and reporting it and interpreting it to the public.

A newspaper job is challenging and rewarding in somewhat the same sense as teaching is challenging and rewarding to many individuals. The basic function of a newspaper is to inform, and informing people means influencing people. Anyone in a position to influence masses of people has a challenging occupation and certainly a responsible one.

A newspaper job offers the opportunity for creative intellectual activity to those who are interested, and my prediction is that the status of the intellectual is rising in our society.

The disadvantages of a newspaper career, from my prejudiced viewpoint, are few. The one most commonly cited is low income. There was a time when this was a legitimate complaint; I doubt that it is now. The median income is higher in some professions than it is among newspapermen, and I hope and expect newspaper salaries will continue to rise, but I think good newspapermen are reasonably well paid. The day is past when a person had to forego a decent income in order to enjoy the pleasures of writing and editing.

As to educational preparation, I always tell high school seniors that if they can afford it they should take four years of straight liberal arts with a fifth year of study in journalism. If they can't afford five years, I recommend four years of liberal arts with some carefully selected journalism courses in the upper two years.

I don't know what to say to a young man who asks how he can tell whether he is qualified for newspaper work. I am always reminded, although I don't

— Photo by *Register* and *Tribune* Staff Photographer Jervas W. Baldwin

Kenneth MacDonald, Editor of the Des Moines *Register* and *Tribune,* glances up from a picture spread on the big football game.

DO YOU BELONG IN JOURNALISM?

admit it, of Louis Armstrong's answer when someone asked him to explain jazz: "If you have to ask you never get to know." I have never thought there was any magic about newspaper talent. It seems to me to be largely a matter of intellectual capacity plus desire. The ability to write understandable prose is not an inborn talent. One of the best reporters I know had difficulty putting a readable sentence together when he began his first newspaper job.

I give the same answers when the questioning senior happens to be a girl, but under those circumstances I am never hopeful of inspiring a fruitful journalistic career. We hire many talented young women. If they would stay with us our newsroom would be a much more attractive place. Unhappily for us, most of them leave in a short time for the joys of marriage and motherhood, and I doubt whether you or I can do much about that.

CHAPTER 17

"Should Like People Reading, Travel, New Experience"

by HOWARD C. HOSMER
Assistant Managing Editor of the Rochester, New York, *Times-Union*

NEWSPAPER WORK OFFERS AS MUCH EXCITEMENT, AS MUCH opportunity, as much satisfaction today as it ever did. Its field for service remains unlimited. Its horizons know no boundaries.

Advantages, both personal and impersonal, are many.

For the individual, there are the satisfactions that come from doing creative, constructive work, from being close to exciting events, from being able to tell people things they want to know, things they should know, from living with the infinite variety life and events offer daily, from being able to benefit from each new experience.

Impersonally, objectively, the advantages are equally numerous. Newspaper work offers an unlimited opportunity for public service, for helping people to know and understand the complexities of modern living, for assisting them in many ways—from an explanation of the tax structure to an explanation of the school bond issue, from the need for a new sewer system to the need for closing a street. In national and international affairs, the issues are broader and more complicated. The same opportunities for service exist. They grow each day. As people become more troubled, more confused, their need for such service multiplies.

Disadvantages in newspaper work are perhaps best judged from the viewpoint of individual personality.

DO YOU BELONG IN JOURNALISM?

The average, normal, intelligent young man or woman who seeks to earn a bundle of money in a hurry, establish a state of affluence quickly, and live in ease and luxury, should not enter it.

It is no business for one who lacks curiosity about people and things, who does not care for reading, who does not care to ask questions, who is not intellectually honest, who is not fair-minded, who bears no tolerance, who is not responsible.

It is no business for one who insists upon regular hours for meals, for sleeping, for leisure, for working. Nor is it a business for one who hopes to close his desk, and his mind, at 5 P.M. and not open either until 8 A.M. the following day.

The dedicated newspaperman lives with his business twenty-four hours a day. The one who does not is working under a disadvantage.

It is no business for the "loner," who cannot work, plan, think, talk with others in the same profession, who is unhappy in close association with his own kind, who thinks of himself rather than the end product, who will neither help nor be helped. Great talent can perhaps overcome such a *modus operandi*, but it is doubtful if it can ever bring much happiness.

It is no business for those who are shoddy, impatient, irresponsible in their personal conduct.

Can a news career be recommended? Yes—for the intellectually curious, the energetic, the persistent, the articulate, the alert. Now, more than ever, besides the opportunities listed above, it offers good pay, security, good working conditions and the happy chances of satisfaction and service.

How do you go about getting into newspaper work? By applying in person to the hiring executive, usually the city editor, news editor or managing editor. By "selling" yourself to him as a good prospect, by showing him through your appearance and conduct that you can meet people and be at ease. By proving to him that you are sincere, that you can write an English sentence, that you are attracted by the opportunities offered in the business rather than by the unimportant, phony, romantic glamour attached to it by those who do not really know it. By proving to him that you think well, speak well and write well enough to transmit your ideas and information clearly to someone else.

What preparation is recommended? If possible, take a full college course

— Photo by *Times-Union* Staff Photographer **Jim Osborne**

Howard C. Hosmer, Assistant Managing Editor of the *Rochester Times-Union*, enjoys a moment of relaxation.

DO YOU BELONG IN JOURNALISM?

in the liberal arts, or a full journalism course with a plentiful liberal arts background.

How can an applicant tell whether he might be qualified? He should want to be a newspaperman more than anything else. It should NOT be his second choice. If it is, the chances are good he will not be happy in it.

He should like people, reading, travel, new experiences. He should like to write and be willing to take criticism. He should be willing to undergo inconvenience. He should inspect himself to see whether he can work under pressure.

He should learn what he is getting into. If this does not discourage him, he has taken a big step. He should appraise his equipment thoroughly and honestly. Does he spell well? Does he have trouble with grammar? Can he remember names? Can he remember dates? Can he remember faces? How well does he organize written material? Is he wordy?

What if the applicant is a girl?

Nearly all of the above applies, with some qualification. (1) If a girl intends to be married early and become a housewife, she should not waste her own or a newspaper's time. (2) If a girl sincerely intends to make it a career, she can make few better choices, economically. As in almost no other business, women in newspaper work have equal opportunities with men, certainly below the executive level.

CHAPTER 18

"To Arrive at Facts and Inform the Public of Them"

by COLEMAN A. HARWELL
Editor of *The Nashville Tennessean*

NEWSPAPERING IS A CAREER WITH RICH OPPORTUNITIES. I KNOW of few things a person can do to give him a greater sense of participation in life.

It is stimulating and challenging. Its variety is endless. It can make use of all the knowledge any man could possibly acquire.

A poor workman or one who does not take pride in his daily tasks is rare in a newsroom today. Almost without exception, every editor and reporter and photographer I know is not only putting out his full effort on today's assignment but is also studying and planning toward improving his effectiveness tomorrow.

I would not recommend it for a person lacking in imagination or dedication. I would recommend it highly for a person who is excited about life's opportunities, who wants to make something better of his own life and who would like to have a hand in making his community and his world a better place to live in.

These are the objects of the minister, the doctor, the lawyer, and should be those of every dedicated person. The object of the newspaperman, in accordance with these aims, is to arrive at facts and inform the public of them. He needs to be conscious of the value and importance of facts—just as a scientist knows that great truths depend upon minute data.

— Photo by *Tennessean* Staff Photographer Bill P

Coleman A. Harwell, Editor of *The Nashville Tennessean,* pauses at the copy desk to examine the world's news moving in by wire.

"To Arrive at Facts and Inform the Public of Them"

The best training, generally, for newspapering, is a broad education. Specifically, the first opportunity presented a youngster is by working on his school publications.

In testing one's capacity, I suggest first of all, good scholarship. It is not essential to be valedictorian of one's class. But the newspaper candidate needs to think clearly, to be able to acquire a great deal of information on a number of subjects and to have intense curiosity about the whys and wherefores of everything.

He needs to be able to write.

It is important that he get along well with other people. There are exceptions, of course, when brilliant people of introverted personalities have made success in positions which do not take them into contact with many people. This is true of many excellent copy editors and news editors. But in most other positions, it is essential to like people.

The economic opportunities in newspapering are above the average. There are instances where talented people could earn more elsewhere than they do in newspaper positions. But this, I believe, is the exception rather than the rule. Many newspapermen with special talents for other work have left newspapering and attained high positions either as executives of corporations or as free-lance authors or in other fields. But in most cities today, I believe the average income of a newspaperman is well above the average of all professional and white-collar people.

My answer for a girl would not vary materially from the above. I would ask her, however, please not to come into my office shining a Phi Beta Kappa key, a sparkling personality and a head full of ideas and then six months later marry the star reporter and turn to the profession she had in mind all the time.

"The First Requirement Is a College Diploma"

CHAPTER 19

by CHARLES STABLER
Managing Editor of the Pacific Coast Edition of *The Wall Street Journal*

WHAT ABOUT NEWSPAPER WORK?

Traditionally, a newspaperman answers that question something like this: "It's a rat race. I'm overworked and underpaid. My editor is a first-class, whip-snapping Simon Legree. And I'm getting an ulcer."

But don't be misled. The newsman is just exercising an age-old prerogative of the trade—grousing about it. Actually, if he's like most newspapermen, he thoroughly enjoys his chosen profession.

By its nature, newspaper work is interesting. It has to be, since it deals with news. Something which isn't interesting isn't news.

In other words, a newspaperman is professionally engaged in seeking out, interpreting and reporting the interesting events and ideas of today's world.

A newsman's work is also varied, as varied as your own newspaper. It ranges from White House press conferences to local school board meetings, from wars to auto wrecks and from high-level financial maneuvering to the rising cost of a T-bone steak.

Of course, you're not likely to be covering the White House one day and the school board the next. But even though you're assigned to a single beat, or area of news, you'll find plenty of diversity. Take the police beat. In a single day you could cover a ripsnorting murder, write a feature on a little girl who got lost and begin to work up an informative article on local theft insurance rates.

"The First Requirement Is a College Diploma"

There is also a variety of jobs to be done on a modern newspaper. They fall into two categories—reporting and editing.

Reporters, of course, dig out the news and either write it up themselves or pass the information along to a rewrite man. They are the eyes and ears of a newspaper and, by extension, of much of the public.

A copy editor checks news stories for accuracy, clarity and completeness. Other editors plan the over-all coverage of the news, making assignments and weighing the relative importance of each day's events.

Another advantage of newspaper work—one which is not generally recognized—is that it offers a wealth of opportunity for qualified people. Despite the traditional difficulty of getting that first job, newspaper editors are constantly on the lookout for promising job candidates. And for a talented reporter or copy reader, there is plenty of chance for advancement.

Right here, let's concede that this is less true for girls than it is for men. There are a good many women in newspaper work, many of them highly successful, but basically a newspaper is still a man's world. Rightly or wrongly, most editors prefer male reporters for most assignments.

Perhaps the single most rewarding facet of journalism is that it is important, giving its workers a feeling of purpose in their daily jobs. Newspapers are, after all, the major mechanism of communication in much of the world. Through newspapers we learn quickly of the problems and progress of our communities and the world around us. Without newspapers, even though we might still have radio, television and magazines, we would find it difficult to deal intelligently with the fast changing complexities of politics, economics and our own lives.

At this point, if you have the native skepticism of a good newspaperman, you're beginning to suspect there must be some flaws in the picture. All right, let's take a candid look at some of the disadvantages of journalism as a career.

Number one on the list is the shortage of high-grade newspapers.

Broadly speaking, a newspaper tries to do two things. It seeks to inform its readers and it seeks to entertain them. Frankly, there are quite a few newspapers which put more emphasis on the entertainment than on information.

Now, there's nothing wrong with entertainment, of course. But most good newspapermen are more interested in facts than in frills. Working on a newspaper which has little interest in developing informed reporting and writing can be mighty discouraging. The best newspapers combine entertainment and information. Their news stories are factual without being grim, fun to read without being too frothy.

When you begin job hunting, start with one like that.

One often-cited disadvantage of journalism is the traditionally low pay scale. In recent years newspaper salaries have shown substantial increases, but the criticism still has some truth. Especially on some of the smaller newspapers, a reporter's life is not likely to be luxurious. On the other hand, many in the profession are drawing very handsome salaries.

Another factor sometimes cited as a disadvantage is the fact that working for a newspaper is not usually a nine to five job. Like a policeman, a reporter is never off duty. And his assigned working hours are likely to be unusual. For example, a police reporter on a morning newspaper will usually come to work at five or six in the evening and work on through to the wee hours. A reporter on an afternoon newspaper starts work early in the morning and checks out in midafternoon.

Thirdly, newspaper work is high pressure. Whether this is considered a disadvantage or not depends on your own temperament. There are people, of course, who choke up under pressure, but many newspapermen find it difficult to work without it. It is not unusual to find a newsman who can't get started writing a story when he has lots of time to do it. But give him a fast-approaching deadline and he'll whip out a finished product in minutes.

Along the same line, newspaper work is highly competitive. There is competition among newspapers; there is competition among the reporters on a single newspaper for the best assignments, the ones most likely to produce major news.

There is also considerable competition among would-be newspapermen for the best jobs. Let's face it. It is not easy to get a reporting post on a major newspaper without previous experience on a smaller one. It can be done and some newspapers, like the one I work for, frequently hire inexperienced men. But the applicant must show truly outstanding potential.

Now then, just how does one go about getting into newspaper work? What preparation is needed?

Charles Stabler, Managing Editor of the Pacific Coast Edition of *The Wall Street Journal*, checks proofs and galleys of type in his San Francisco composing room.

DO YOU BELONG IN JOURNALISM?

Practically speaking, the first requirement is a college diploma. To be sure, there are a good many men in the profession who did not go to college. But they are becoming more rare and a present-day applicant without a B.A. starts his job hunting with two strikes against him. As for grades, they don't have to be A's but they ought to be fairly close to it.

One question which often arises concerning college is whether you should go to journalism school. It is difficult to answer flatly yes or no, largely because it makes very little difference.

The really important consideration is what you learn, not where you learn it.

Journalism school will introduce you to some of the lingo and basic techniques of the profession. Usually you'll have an opportunity to meet working members of the press at lectures. And most journalism schools have a placement service which can provide real assistance in finding a job after you get your sheepskin.

But, with all this, the best journalism schools actually teach very little in the way of straight how-to-do-it courses. Usually vocational subjects make up less than a third of your total course load. Instead, you are encouraged to study a variety of subjects—history, political science, economics and the like.

The reason for this is obvious. As a reporter you'll be covering a broad variety of issues and events. The greater your backlog of knowledge, the better reporter you'll be.

As you progress in newspaper work, you'll find yourself specializing in certain types of news. For example, even though most reporters start on "general assignment," they eventually work into concentrating on such subjects as local politics, labor, business and financial news, sports and the like. But you'll still find a broad background of knowledge helpful.

So, if you go to journalism school, study as many nonjournalism subjects as you can cram in.

If, on the other hand, you decide against journalism school and take a straight liberal arts course, try to get an introduction to the profession.

One means of doing this is to work on your college newspaper. There you'll have an opportunity to do some copy editing, headline writing and reporting.

Another and perhaps more useful source of training is your college news

"The First Requirement Is a College Diploma"

bureau or press relations office. This office reports on college activities for newspapers in its community. You'll be covering sports events, reporting speeches by visitors and so on. The advantage of taking part in this activity is that you will be working with regular newspapers, learning their needs and style.

If your college doesn't have such a bureau, try being one yourself. Call up the city editor of the local newspaper and tell him you'd like a tryout as a "college correspondent." If he takes you on as a "stringer," you'll find the job has another big plus mark: You get paid for it. Moreover, such a job can be the opening wedge for a full-time post after graduation.

Any summer vacation newspaper experience you can acquire will be tremendously helpful later on. It will help you to decide whether you've made a correct choice of career. And it will arm you with clippings when you start job hunting after commencement.

Don't be discouraged if the summer job is rather lowly. You have a lot to learn and the bottom is generally considered a good place to start your education.

One thing more. The English language will be the basic tool of your trade. Treat it with respect. It may seem like small stuff, but if you haven't already learned grammar and spelling, devote some of your college time to doing so.

This will save you some embarrassment and your future editor some headaches. Consider, for example, this true tale:

A former police reporter on the *Richmond Times-Dispatch* had chronic difficulty with the kinship of survivors listed in an obituary. He was forever writing "brother-in-laws" and "sister-in-laws."

But at long last the city editor was able to drill into him that it should be "brothers-in-law" and so on.

"O.K., I think I've got it," said the reporter proudly—and then handed in an obituary which read: "Joe Zilch, 70, died yesterday. He was an ardent sportsman and lover of the outs-of-door."

Silly? All right then, quickly, which is correct? "Everyone else's" or "everyone's else."

And don't neglect your vocabulary. Do you know for certain what "shambles" means? Or "replica?" Or "virtually?"

DO YOU BELONG IN JOURNALISM?

What all this adds up to is this: Prepare yourself for a career in journalism by, first, acquiring a broad background in liberal arts and other subjects; second, making sure you know the proper usage of English, and third, trying to get some actual newspaper experience.

Aside from all that, what else does it take to be a good reporter? Plenty. But before going into it, here's a word of advice: Don't be discouraged if you don't think you can meet all the qualifications.

For one reason, they're a matter of opinion, not infallible. For a second, not many reporters—very few, in fact—could be rated perfect. But they're often able to be successful reporters, in spite of that. For example, a man's writing may be weak but he can still be valuable in digging out facts.

With that in mind, how would you rate yourself on the following characteristics? Good, bad or so-so?

Perception and insight. Things are not always what they seem. As a reporter you'll be looking for hidden motives, deeper meanings to surface actions and statements. You'll be looking for the true significance of the events you report, the "why" and the "so what."

Curiosity. Are you interested in what's happening in the world and your home town? Why it's happening? What it means for the future? A good reporter has an insatiable appetite for information.

Clarity. You'll have to write clearly and that means you'll have to think clearly. Can you make sense out of complex situations?

Accuracy. No matter how deathless your prose, it won't do a newspaper reader much good if he can't trust your statement of the facts.

Speed. And, even if the story is accurate, it's no good if it's written too late.

Resourcefulness. Many stories, especially the best ones, will require you to get information which may be deliberately concealed. More and more, secrecy is a problem for newspapers and, for that matter, the public. If you're locked out of a City Planning Commission meeting, you'll have to find ways of digging out what happened there. Your city editor will want a story, not an explanation of why you didn't get one.

There's another characteristic of good reporters which is more difficult to describe. In effect, it's the ability to develop news sources and contacts,

"The First Requirement Is a College Diploma"

so called. But more than that, it's a genuine interest in people, a desire to talk to them, to know them and understand their actions.

This does not mean a reporter has to be a backslapper and glad-hander. Nor does it mean that he kowtows to his news sources. But he is able to inspire confidence in himself, winning the trust of other people so they will talk to him freely and honestly.

To sum up all this, a reporter gets the news, gets it right and makes it public while it is still news. And with all, a sense of humor won't do you any harm.

No outsider can tell in advance whether or not you have the qualities which go into making a good reporter. That's something you'll have to assess for yourself and it will pay you to do it honestly.

Well, all right. You have decided you want to make a career of journalism, you think you have the potential for success and you've done all you can in advance preparation. What next?

Get a job, obviously, but how and where?

First, you'll have to decide whether you want to start with a large newspaper or a small one. There are advantages to both, and disadvantages.

On a large newspaper, you'll probably go into some sort of preliminary training. On many, this means working as a copy boy and trying to absorb information in your spare time. On others, you'll work for a time with experienced reporters, finding out how they operate and handle their beats. This is on-the-job training under close supervision and guidance.

On a smaller newspaper you'll have an opportunity to tackle a greater variety of stories. And you'll probably begin getting good assignments sooner than you would on a large newspaper. On the other hand, your training may not be quite as good.

Actually, of course, you may not have a choice. You may find that opportunities for starting jobs on the larger newspapers are so limited that you'll have to begin with a small one. Don't let this discourage you; that's where many top newspapermen started and, for that matter, there are still many good ones who stay on small newspapers out of their own preference.

Applying for a newspaper position is much like applying for work anywhere. On a large newspaper, you'll probably start with the personnel office.

DO YOU BELONG IN JOURNALISM?

On a small one, start with the managing editor. Apply to as many newspapers as possible and don't be limited by geography; if you can't get a post in your home town, try somewhere else.

Be persistent. It's difficult for a newspaper to forecast its hiring needs. An editor who tells you one week that he has no openings may be looking hard for a good man the next month. Don't let him forget you.

Don't mail in your clippings, if you have any, because they may get lost. But bring them to an interview. If you have not had an opportunity to do any newspaper work and have no clippings, bring along other material you've written. An editor can get a reasonably good idea of your writing and organization of material from a term paper, even though it's not done in newspaper style.

Ask questions. The editor will want to know how well developed your bump of curiosity is. And you'll want to know more about the newspaper.

Once you're on a newspaper, you'll be judged chiefly by your product. You'll be expected to cover the news and report it quickly and clearly. If you do that, you'll have no need to worry about your job security or future advancement. One of the nice things about newspaper work is that you are judged by your performance, not your skill at office politics.

And you'll always have a pretty fair notion of how you're doing. If your stories are getting in the paper without too much rewriting, if you know what's happening on your beat without reading the opposition newspaper and you're getting a steady flow of bylines, you're doing all right.

And there's nothing like it. To see something you wrote in print with your name at the top is a thrill which will never leave you.

CPSIA information can be obtained
at www.ICGtesting.com
Printed in the USA
LVHW101629071118
596304LV00010BA/425/P